RYAN'S STORY

A FATHER'S HARD-EARNED LESSONS ABOUT CYBERBULLYING AND SUICIDE

JOHN P. HALLIGAN
EMILY B. DICKSON

CONTENTS

Dedicated

to

Sister Mary Laurena Cullen

The names of the persons in this story who bullied Ryan have been changed to protect their privacy. This is a story about forgiveness, not blame. I want these individuals to forgive themselves, as I have forgiven them.

John Halligan

INTRODUCTION

On October 7, 2003, I lost my thirteen-year-old son, Ryan, to suicide. It was revealed in greater detail, after Ryan's death, that he was ridiculed and humiliated by his peers at his Vermont middle school and online. I decided to channel all the pain and anger of what happened to Ryan into something constructive, and quite frankly therapeutic too. I knew more education and prevention was needed in our schools. I didn't want other families to feel the kind of pain I was experiencing. In 2004, I spearheaded the Vermont Bullying Prevention law in honor of Ryan. In 2006, I then led the passing of a law which requires education about suicide prevention in public schools.

In the spring of 2005, I received a phone call from Judy Breitmeyer, a counselor at Mount Mansfield Union High School in Jericho, Vermont. She told me that her student leadership team was planning a "Respect Day" and they wanted to have a kickoff assembly with me as the keynote speaker. They had followed my work during the prior year in passing the Vermont Bullying Prevention law and thought it would be great to have me come and tell Ryan's story to the whole student body. I replied, "I have not been in front of high school students since I was in high school. No offense, but that audience can be a bit challenging in holding their attention!" She implored me just to give it a try, reassuring me that they would be attentive and respectful.

I reluctantly agreed because I still wasn't sure what to say to these students. After many days of stressing over how to tell Ryan's story, I decided to just speak from my heart and then let the students ask questions at the end.

On May 11, 2005, I gave the presentation for the first time – Ryan's Story was born. As I paused in between sentences, the audience was silent; you could hear a pin drop. As I looked at the audience, I saw many eyes welling up with tears. I could sense the students were connecting with the story. When the presentation was over, the audience gave me a standing ovation and several students came up to shake my hand and even hug me. The response was overwhelming. I had never experienced anything like this before and sensed something unusual had happened that morning. Sure enough, by word of mouth and through social media, other Vermont schools learned about my well-received presentation and urged me to come to their schools.

In this time frame, I was also invited to share Ryan's Story on several national TV programs, including

Oprah, *Primetime with Diane Sawyer*, and PBS *Frontline*. Well, those appearances created an explosion of emails, many from school administrators from around the country begging me to come to speak to their students. In February 2009, I decided to end my very secure and successful career at IBM and take the risk of becoming a full-time motivational speaker. Since then, I have been to over two thousand schools throughout the United States, Canada, and Mexico spreading Ryan's Story and the messages of forgiveness, kindness, and hope.

I have received thousands of emails and handwritten letters from students expressing how much this presentation affected them. So often the students tell me that Ryan's Story changed their life for the better. So many have even confessed they were the bully and apologized to the victim. And many targets of bullying shared with me that they gained the courage to get help from adults. Countless others expressed they will no longer be a bystander to bullying but have chosen to be an upstander.

Along the way, I started getting requests to offer a presentation for parents. At first, I thought I would give the same presentation I was giving to the students. But then I thought, no, this has to be different. I needed to provide parent-specific information and share the hard lessons learned as a parent in this predicament. At first, it was hard to admit the parenting mistakes I made. But as I continued to share, rather than receiving criticism, I received countless emails of gratitude. Parents appreciated my openness, honesty, and practical advice. The only challenge that continues to face me to this day is not being able to reach every parent within a school community. Too often, like any other school-sponsored events for parents, the turnout is typically low. Although I have been told over the years, my attendance is higher than average because after the students hear me during the day, they have urged their parents to see Mr. Halligan's presentation in the evening. The parents that did come, often express they wished every parent saw my presentation.

So, with the hope of casting my net out further, I decided to write this book. It contains everything I share in my presentation with a lot more detail of Ryan's story and additional advice I don't have time to fit into the hour and a half I have with the parents. But I also was mindful to keep this book short and to the point with practical advice since time is a scarce commodity for parents with school-age children and demanding careers.

I also recognized I would benefit significantly by teaming up with a middle school counselor with years of real-life experiences in facing these issues of mental health, relationship problems, and the role technology has played over the years. Even more ideal would be someone with her own school-age children soon to be in the middle school years. I met Emily Dickson at her middle school in Southington, Connecticut in the fall of 2017. She had invited me to the district to share Ryan's Story with her students and their parents. In between presentations we discussed in great detail ongoing issues and her own challenges as a parent of a six-year-old and a nine-year-old already asking for a cell phone. I was relieved to hear her say she knows access was not appropriate at this age and expressed her plan to delay it beyond middle school. She saw first-hand the damage these devices cause to the psychological and emotional well-being of her students. I found the perfect co-author for my book! Emily has proven to be a valuable contributor. She is to be credited with not only improving my writing style (engineers are notoriously bad at this) but also contributing sound practical advice when it comes to depression and suicidal expressions by a child. I am so grateful for Emily's help in making this an even better book for parents.

I am also grateful you decided to pick up this book and to take this heart wrenching but also inspiring journey, so you may learn from my tragic loss and gain additional insight to do what is best for your child. God bless you and your family.

PROLOGUE

IT WAS 6 a.m. I was asleep in my hotel room in Rochester, New York during a business trip for IBM when the phone rang and jolted me awake. It was my wife, Kelly.

"John, you need to come home! You need to come home! Ryan hanged himself!"

"He… is he all right?" My brain was trying to process what Kelly was saying to me.

"No, John. Our son is dead. He killed himself!"

Time stopped.

It can't be true.

Kelly would tell you I hung up on her. I actually dropped my flip phone in horror and the battery popped out of the back, disconnecting the call. I just stood there frozen in time, praying I would just suddenly wake up from this nightmare.

There is no way he is dead. I just saw him yesterday.

I couldn't accept that I would never hear his voice again, never see his smile again, never hold him again. *No, this can't be!*

Then it hit me... hard: the conversation we had about a week earlier when Ryan expressed his thought about suicide because he was not doing well at school and felt he was a "loser."

At the end of a long conversation, one I thought was productive, we hugged and he said, "Dad, promise you won't tell Mom about our conversation? I don't want to go back to that therapist. It was a waste of time."

"Okay, I promise."

I thought he just needed a pep talk. My God, I messed up. It's all my fault. Our son is dead and it's all my fault.

1

WE ARE GOING TO BE OKAY HERE

IT WAS the black-and-white electric Johnson Stratocaster guitar he had asked for and I couldn't wait to see his face when he got home from his lesson to see it. I had his initials, R.P.H., engraved in red letters on the body and placed it upright in the front room already hooked up to a brand-new amplifier.

Ryan had decided that he wanted to learn to play guitar only a month earlier, and he was enthusiastically taking private lessons with a young man in Burlington, Vermont. It was great to see him find something that he was passionate about. Kelly, my wife, had bought him an acoustic guitar and a bunch of beginner books. Ryan was eager to learn songs by his favorite bands: Green Day, Good Charlotte, Atticus, Dropkick Murphys, and blink-182. His music teacher encouraged him to bring the songs that he wanted to learn to play. He recognized that having Ryan hear himself play these songs, with a bit of typical beginner's clumsiness, would keep him motivated. Kelly and I loved to spy on him as he practiced in the front room of our colonial-style home. I was so proud of him as he was showing great potential in mastering a musical instrument. The only instrument I had ever mastered was the "air" guitar.

As the month went by, Ryan's focus on guitar playing provided him with a necessary boost of confidence. So, when he came to me one day in October and asked me to look at an electric guitar for sale on eBay, he said, "Dad, I would be so happy if you bought this for me." How could I resist? Although he enjoyed the acoustic guitar, most of his favorite bands featured the electric guitar. And he wanted to be just like them.

UPS delivered the package on October 4, 2003. You would have thought it was Christmas morning by his excitement. Immediately, Ryan started to try out some of his favorite riffs. He and a few of his friends planned to start a punk rock band. This was just what he needed to feel accepted and important.

I had no idea that this would be the last gift I'd ever give my son. I didn't realize that this would be the last music lesson he'd ever take or the last week of his life.

Ryan was our second child. His sister, Megan, was three years older than he was. At the time of Megan's birth, my wife and I were young newlyweds who did not exactly intend to become parents so quickly. I had just graduated with my engineering degree, and Kelly had just finished nursing school. We were still in the stage of our lives when all of our friends were going out to bars on weeknights and, suddenly, we were thrust into the role of becoming responsible adults. We did our absolute best to play the part. There would be no more starting our weekends on a Thursday night and coming home from the bars at 2 a.m. Now, it seemed to be our duty as dedicated parents to get to bed early because parenting demanded a lot more energy and patience during the day.

Megan had been a colicky baby, which had made it a bit challenging for us to get a good night's sleep. However, her crying fits did not last long, and she hit all of her developmental milestones as expected of a healthy child. Kelly and I wanted our children to be close enough in age so that they could play with one another. As a result, Ryan's birth on December 18, 1989 was planned. His birth was the best Christmas gift. We invited the whole family over to celebrate. A girl and a boy – what more could you ask for?

In many ways, Ryan was an easy baby. He was sweet and cheerful and the kind of baby everyone wanted to hold and hug. But, when it came to the developmental milestones, Ryan seemed to be behind. Crawling, standing, and walking were all significantly delayed developmental milestones for Ryan. He was behind schedule and seemed uncoordinated. However, the larger issue was that at the age of two, he still wasn't talking. He didn't speak a single word, not even "Mama" or "Dada." I was concerned, but only mildly so.

"You didn't talk until kindergarten!" my mother reminded me. In fact, that was a story I heard often.

Back in the late 1960s, my kindergarten teacher even wrote on my report card that it seemed as if I was just learning to talk for the first time. My parents were not too worried about my delayed communication. There was more of a nonchalant attitude about these things. "Let's just wait and see" was the family doctor's advice. Once I began talking, I caught up quickly to the other kids. So my mother assured me that the same thing would happen with Ryan. "He's probably just saving it up," she said. I can remember thinking that I looked forward to all he was going to say one day.

Kelly started bringing Ryan to a local hospital twice a week for speech therapy. However, the pediatrician was more concerned when Ryan turned three years old and still wasn't talking or understanding words the way most other children were. He did a lot of nonsensical babbling, but older sister Megan did most of the talking for him. Therefore, the doctor sent us for an evaluation at the local elementary school. It was through this evaluation that we officially found out that our son had delays with speech and language, and gross and fine motor skills. As a result of the evaluation, he would qualify for early intervention speech services and occupational therapy in preschool.

At first, a yellow bus came to pick Ryan up for preschool twice a week. Then, we soon increased to school every day. He climbed onto the bus fearlessly and always came home with a big smile on his face. I was amazed at how cheerful he was throughout this period of time – while we became more worried about his learning issues and fearful about the potential for a difficult academic future. But, to Ryan, learning truly seemed to be an adventure which he was eager to face every day.

We were so thankful for Ryan's teachers in Pough-keepsie, New York. They were angels to us. They were incredibly caring and reassuring, not only to Ryan, but to Kelly and I as concerned parents. Under their angelic wings, we finally got to hear our sweet son begin to speak and sing his favorite song, "Wheels on the Bus." We were not sure this would ever happen, so it was truly music to our ears. I felt so relieved to hear the sound of Ryan's voice forming coherent words. I thought, "Perhaps his academic future will be fine after all."

The success Ryan had with his teachers was why it was so hard to deal with the news we received in February of 1993 – there was going to be a big change in our lives. I was working for IBM at the time, and the company was going through a very difficult period. Thousands of my coworkers in the Hudson Valley region were being laid off. I easily could have been one of them, but I was offered an alternative. I could continue to work for IBM if I relocated to a manufac-turing plant in Essex Junction, Vermont. Kelly and I were relieved that I still had a job; there had been some tense months where we didn't know if I would. Although I wasn't happy to uproot my family, there wasn't much of a choice. If I wanted to keep my job, it meant picking up and moving to a state where we had no connections. But I had been to this site several times prior for business trips and I was familiar with the area.

It was on a snowy Valentine's Day when I first showed Kelly around Market Street in downtown Burlington. I knew Kelly would love Vermont. The view of the Congregational Church, which is at the end of the street, is lined with restaurants, bars, and shops. There are always plenty of people walking around as it is an iconic landmark of Vermont. There are many paintings and pictures that mimic this scene. It is most beautiful during the holiday season with the Christmas tree lit up in front of the church. The area is populated mostly with people of French and Irish descent. There-fore, culturally, I knew we would fit in easily with a name like "Halligan."

We had to move fast with the house hunting since my first day at the Vermont IBM plant was set for April 1st. Based on the realtor's and my co-workers' input, we decided to focus on Essex Junction, since the school district was highly recommended, especially for students with special needs. We found a nice, simple raised ranch–style house on a cul-de-sac. This was ideal for raising young children since speeding cars and heavy through traffic was not even possible on this short dead end. Once we went into contract on the house, we set up a meeting at Megan and Ryan's new school, Hiawatha Elementary. The school was conveniently just a half-mile walk from our new home, with a crossing guard for the one busy street they would have to cross.

We were immediately impressed with the teachers

and administration. The principal, Peter Hunt, was a very kind and dedicated man who loved his school. (He would later retire and successfully run for public office to become our state representative. Peter became the lead sponsor of my bullying prevention bill and was instrumental in getting it passed.) It was of utmost importance to us to meet with the special education team and establish the IEP (Individualized Education Plan) for Ryan. We were pleased to find them to be very dedicated and experienced professionals with a love for their school and students. But only time would tell if this was a good move for us, and especially for Ryan.

Before long, I sighed with relief. The special education teachers at Hiawatha Elementary School were just as wonderful as the teachers at his former school. By the time kindergarten started he was in a mainstream regular education class and was pulled out several times a week for special education services. Kids at that age didn't seem to care or notice. Many other kids also got pulled out for special education services, so it wasn't a big deal. Ryan made friends easily and seemed genuinely happy. His very sweet, sensitive soul started to show itself. I thought to myself, we are going to be okay here after all.

2

THANK YOU FOR BEING THE NORMAL ONE

IN THE EARLY elementary school years, Ryan developed an interest in sports: baseball, soccer, and basketball. He wanted us to sign him up for everything. He was so excited about it, so how could we refuse? We loved his enthusiasm. He seemed to enjoy the social aspect of sports the most – having the opportunity to be with his friends. Even though he still had motor delays, the positive thing about the elementary age group is that they are all learning a sport for the first time. Everyone looks a bit goofy. So Ryan didn't stand out too much, and he did not get made fun of either. It seemed as if the other kids did not notice that he was different. However, a neighbor did turn to me once and say, "He seems awkward." It wasn't a simple observation; I could tell by her tone that it was judgmental. "Thanks, lady," I thought. For the first time, I felt hurt by the stinging words of a fellow parent about my child. "Yeah, well, he still has a lot of growing up to do," I stumbled in reply.

Although it was sad to leave our extended family behind and only be able to have our children see their grandparents a couple of times a year, everyone seemed to be adjusting well to Vermont. Our family had another big adjustment that same year: to our surprise, Kelly got pregnant again. We had our third and final child, Conor, when Ryan was seven. He was so proud to be a big brother! You could see it all over Ryan's face. It was wonderful to watch him interact with the baby. He was gentle, loving, and would grow to become very protective of Conor.

Conor developed like a typical baby until about the age of two, when he gradually regressed. He wasn't talking, which we were not too shocked or worried about because we had been down this path before with Ryan. However, Conor's tantrums became more extreme as time went on. We had seen the "terrible twos" before, but nothing like this. At times, Conor would get very violent. For example, there were times when he would throw a glass or knock over a lamp with the clear intention of breaking it.

"Mom, I think something's wrong with Conor," Ryan said one day in the middle of one of Conor's tantrums. Ryan was a perceptive kid, and it took him saying it out loud for us to acknowledge that Conor might be going through something more than just a stage. Conor wasn't interested in interacting with anyone or anything. When we visited our next-door neighbor, all Conor wanted to do was keep changing the speed of their ceiling fan in the living room the entire visit. They could have brought in a dozen puppies, and he'd just want to stare at that ceiling fan. He seemed obsessed. We knew something wasn't right.

As we did with Ryan, we had Conor evaluated at age three. He was diagnosed with PDD NOS (Pervasive Developmental Disorder Not Otherwise Specified), a diagnosis often assigned when the evaluator does not believe a child has all of the "ingredients" to be labeled autistic. Conor's terrible twos lasted for years. This added a lot of stress to our household and meant that we spent a disproportionate amount of time focused on Conor's needs.

During this same period, Megan began to have difficulty with her friend group, and when she began middle school, things reached a boiling point for the family. For the first time, Megan experienced the "mean girl" syndrome. For example, one particular girl in her group of friends would turn on her every so often and make nasty comments to her face and behind her back. This same girl would then spread rumors about Megan and tell the other girls not to sit with her in the cafeteria.

Megan began to take out her anger and frustration at home on her mom. She would talk about her friend issues almost every day after school, a discussion that often left her in tears. Kelly would always offer her advice about how Megan could handle the situation, often by encouraging Megan to find new friends. Megan would get upset with her for even suggesting this, screaming, "You don't understand!" Kelly and I were both at a loss as to how to help Megan with her peer conflicts, especially since she did not want to take most of our advice.

During this period, the balancing act of being a parent to all of our children had become much more challenging and overwhelming for both Kelly and I. One day, Kelly was in the middle of dealing with one of Conor's out-of-control tantrums when Megan burst into the room wanting to be heard. Kelly was trying to give Megan her undivided attention, while simultaneously trying to calm Conor's tantrum. "Pay attention to me!" Megan yelled with her arms flailing. Kelly looked up and there was Ryan with a big grin on his face. He was eating a Zebra Cake, his favorite treat, and found this moment highly entertaining. Kelly put her hands on both of Ryan's cheeks and said, "Thank you for being my normal one."

Megan began to see a therapist to help her deal with the social issues that she was experiencing. Her problems sounded petty to our adult ears, but to a preteen, they were devastating. While in therapy, Megan was clinically diagnosed with OCD (Obsessive Compulsive Disorder), which was in turn part of the reason why she was having friend issues.

Megan's struggles with OCD were largely invisible to her peers, and yet she was still having difficulties. I worried that Ryan's status as a special education student would mean that his experience in middle and high school would be even more difficult than Megan's. Ryan wasn't athletic or academically strong, both of which I knew could cause problems for him. I was especially worried about his lack of athletic skills since there is such a big emphasis on playing sports when it comes to boys. What he did have going for him was his kind personality. Many kids genuinely liked him. Most parents liked him too. I beamed with parental pride when one of his friend's mothers told me that she welcomed the days when Ryan came over to visit. "I hope some of his sweetness rubs off on my son," she said.

Ryan was also kind to us, his family. He very rarely got angry or threw a fit over something. He also started to show more and more of his sensitive side. He often expressed worry for his little brother, wondering if he would ever be "normal." He was an excellent big brother to Conor. At an age when most kids don't want anything to do with their little siblings, Ryan remained ever patient with Conor. For example, Conor would often bang on Ryan's bedroom door when Ryan and his friends were playing with the Xbox. We would hear Ryan's friends say, "Please don't let him in," but Ryan would open the door every time. No matter what his friends wanted him to do, he always thought about his little brother's feelings. He was such a loving, sweet, sensitive, and good-natured kid. Unfortunately, his sensitivity would become one of the reasons why he started to get bullied.

I hoped his kindness would have a protective effect against being bullied but, even so, I was worried. As he approached the middle school years, I could see that the close friends he made were not likely going to be the jocks or the popular kids. They were, for the most part, goofy like Ryan was. They would get together to play video games and watch television shows, such as *Malcolm in the Middle*. Most of his friends were more musically inclined than academically inclined. And, unfortunately, Ryan was becoming aware of the social order that existed in school. He realized that he and his close friends were different and began to view these differences as deficiencies. It was no longer easy for Ryan to play sports now that most of the kids had become more skilled than he had. He still wanted to play, but he knew he wasn't very good. Therefore, Ryan made the decision to give up on sports. However, he did remain very close friends with an athletic boy, named Raphael, who was from our neighborhood. I thought and hoped this friendship might provide Ryan some protective cover from bullies.

Each year, Ryan had to be retested for the special education services he received in school. At the end of the fourth grade, we got a terrific report. The evaluator felt that his speech and language skills had caught up to grade level and, as a result, he no longer needed to be pulled out of the classroom for special education services. We were thrilled for many different reasons. We were happy to hear that he had made such good progress and were also relieved that he would get to ditch the "SPED" label before middle school. Ryan was particularly happy about that as well since he was just beginning to become aware of how the SPED label was negatively referred to by some of his peers.

We headed into the summer with the highest of hopes. Kelly and I truly believed that fifth grade was going to be Ryan's best year ever.

3

THE BULLYING BEGINS AND ENDS, SO WE THOUGHT

"HE CALLS ME 'SPED KID'!" Ryan announced to us with distress. "Even though I'm not even in SPED anymore. He makes fun of me in gym class. No one wants to choose me for their team because of him." I thought to myself, "Here we go again with the awful middle school years. Now it's Ryan's turn."

I felt bad my own son didn't inherit my athletic capabilities. I was a weak student academically, but through sports I was able to deflect the focus away from my academic performance. I was able to gain the respect of others since I was a better than average athlete, especially in football. It was during the middle school years that Ryan began to feel inadequate amongst his peers. Understanding this now, I feel guilty for showing Ryan the old photographs of me in my baseball and football uniforms. I also feel guilty for having my childhood athletic awards displayed throughout our family den. I still wonder to this day if these two things made him feel as if he needed to live up to certain athletic expectations.

The "he" who Ryan was complaining about was a boy named Mason (as stated in the Author's Note, this name has been changed). Mason had been somewhat friendly with Ryan until the fifth grade, when things changed between them. He had made derogatory comments here and there towards Ryan, throughout the years, which alerted us that he was a troublemaker and possibly a bully. For example, Ryan's third grade teacher would post the progress each student made with the multiplication times table for the class to see. Looking back on this now, it does not seem like an appropriate thing for a teacher to do. Mason would often make snide comments about how far behind Ryan was with his work in comparison to the other students in his class. Now, in the fifth grade, things suddenly escalated and took a turn for the worse. Mason had it in for Ryan – big time.

I sat Ryan down and we talked about Mason and how he had been treating Ryan. "Okay, let's figure this out. Mason probably has a lot of issues of his own. Maybe he has a difficult family life, has frustrations built up about it, and is looking for someone at school to take it out on. Kids like this just want to see a reaction. If you give him any kind of response, show a tear or any emotion, he'll keep at it. You need to ignore this kid. Just walk away. He'll get bored and move on to someone else," I said.

Ignore the bully and he'll go away. This was the

standard, time-tested parental advice. "I guess. I'll try," mumbled Ryan. My advice to Ryan was easier to give than it was to take. Ryan continued to have emotional outbursts about how Mason focused on Ryan's perceived shortcomings. Ryan would often start complaining immediately on the way home from school with Kelly. One day, Kelly asked Ryan if he thought it might be helpful for him to speak to someone other than his parents for advice. Ryan agreed that seeing a therapist might be helpful, so we asked our pediatrician for a recommendation.

In January of 2001, Ryan began seeing his therapist weekly for the next six months. When Kelly was younger, her parents pried too much into her personal life (including the ultimate betrayal of reading her diary!). Therefore, she always maintained the opposite tactic with parenting our children. Kelly didn't pry or snoop at all. After Ryan's therapy sessions, she'd ask him how it went and Ryan would always say "fine," or some variation thereof, and that would be the end of the conversation. Sometimes Ryan would volunteer information, such as he and the therapist played chess during the session. However, what they talked about and what advice the therapist gave to him remained a mystery to us. We made the decision to respect the therapeutic process and leave their sessions between the two of them.

Feeling as if we needed to do more, Kelly and I decided to speak with Ryan's teacher, Mr. Gazo. He was a caring man who really liked Ryan. Mr. Gazo promised to keep an eye on Ryan and address any situation immediately. He became Ryan's fifth grade guardian angel. With both the therapy sessions and Mr. Gazo's watchful eye, over the course of the next few months, things improved.

By the end of the fifth grade, we stopped hearing about Ryan being bullied and his depression seemed to have lifted. We were satisfied that things were stable and that Ryan was in a better place emotionally.

Sixth grade was fairly uneventful. Once in a while, Ryan mentioned Mason. Although Ryan spoke less frequently of Mason, we found out through a parent of one of Ryan's friends that Mason was becoming more physically aggressive with some of his classmates. A few times, Ryan mentioned that Mason had given him a shove during gym class. In my eyes, this seemed like typical boy behavior, so I was not overly concerned. For the most part, Ryan seemed to have learned how to brush off Mason's behavior. Ryan's sister, Megan, was now in high school and she often told him, "Hang in there. It gets a lot better when you get to high school. We are a lot more mature and a lot of the middle school nonsense stops."

We all thought that the worst of it was behind us, which is why his meltdown in December of his seventh-grade year completely blindsided us.

"He's been like this all afternoon. He won't talk to anyone," Kelly said. Ryan was sitting at the kitchen table with his head down and he was not moving. I put my arm around him and tried to convince him to speak with me. Finally, he exploded.

"I *HATE* that school. I hate it there and I never want to go back! Can you homeschool me? Can we move?"

"Ryan, what is going on here? Where is this coming from? What's wrong with school?" I pleaded with him for more information.

We hadn't heard a word about Ryan being bullied since the year had started, so we were blown away when Ryan revealed that he was having problems again with Mason and his friends. This time, however, he thought he was supposed to handle his problems himself. After all, he was thirteen years old and a full-fledged teenager. He thought it was immature to ask Mom and Dad for help. So, he had bottled this up during the first few months of seventh grade.

"I'm going to call the guidance counselor and the principal first thing tomorrow and we're going to put an end to this once and for all," I said.

"No! Don't do that," Ryan yelled. "You know that'll just make it worse!"

"Then I'm going to call this kid's parents and talk to them."

"No! That would embarrass me even more."

At this point I was getting impatient with Ryan. "Look, in terms of your request, homeschooling is not an option. Mom works part-time, and we can't have her just quit her job and make this happen overnight. Moving to a new school district is not a quick solution either. It's the middle of winter in Vermont. If we put the house up for sale now, it probably won't sell until the spring. We need to come up with a plan to deal with this kid now."

I could tell that Ryan was thinking about what I had just said and trying to come up with a solution. After a few minutes he said, "You know what, Dad? I want you to teach me how to fight. I need to know how to defend myself. I know it's been mostly words, but I'm really afraid this kid and his friends are going to try to do something to me and I just want to be able to defend myself."

The movie *The Karate Kid* flashed through my mind – teenage Daniel being taught how to fight by Mr. Miyagi so that he could fend off the popular bully, Johnny, and the rest of the Cobra Kai. Ryan asking me to teach him how to fight made me feel like Mr. Miyagi. I thought about the scene where Daniel knocks out Johnny and teaches him a lesson. I thought that it would be pretty funny to see that happen in Ryan's case. He laughed when I told him that, but he wasn't interested in learning karate.

"I want to learn Tae Bo kickboxing," he said. That year, Billy Blanks was all over television promoting his many video exercise programs: *Tae Bo Classic*, *Tae Bo Extreme!*, and *Billy's Bootcamp: Cardio Inferno*. Ryan was mesmerized by this guy. He would sit and watch the entire infomercial whenever it came on. "Can I have the kickboxing program for Christmas? Not just the video, but also the big red kickboxing bag and the red boxing gloves?" he asked. I told him that I would talk with his mother about it.

Not only did I talk to Kelly, but I also checked in with a few of my friends. Was I doing the right thing here? Was it just encouraging him to use violence to solve a problem?

Everyone reassured me that this was a really good decision. Ryan would get in better shape, build his confidence, and learn self-defense all at the same time. Most of all, it allowed for some extra father and son bonding time as I found myself doing the exercises with him.

Right after the holidays, we got into a routine every night after dinner and homework. We would go into the basement, put on the red boxing gloves, and do Tae Bo together. Not only did we exercise together every night, we also had a lot of time to talk. We talked about everything – what he was doing at school, my own experiences with bullies, and our thoughts about the future.

"Ryan, what do you want to be when you grow up?" I asked. Ryan's answer was always the same, "An actor and a comedian." He loved to tell funny stories and make people laugh. He was good at it and I was glad that he had future plans for himself.

After a month or so, Ryan started to get pretty good at Tae Bo kickboxing and I felt the need to sit him down and have a serious talk with him. "You know the uppercut, the crossover, and the jab. You have all these boxing moves down and that's great. But the last thing I want to happen is for us to get a call from the school that you are becoming a bully. I don't want to hear that you are starting fights because you *know* how to fight. I don't ever want to get that phone call. But if Mason or any of his friends ever lay a single finger on you, you have my full permission to whale on him. Teach him a lesson. Just like in *The Karate Kid*."

Sure enough, the call from the school came just a few weeks later in February of 2003. The assistant principal called to tell my wife that he had heard a rumor throughout the school day that there was going to be a big fight at the Maple Street Park, which was just down the road from the middle school.

The assistant principal told us that when he got there, there was a fight well underway between Ryan and Mason. "I don't know how long they had been fighting, but I broke it up and checked on your son. Ryan seems to be okay, with no visible injuries. I just want you to know that this happened," he told us.

Kelly called me immediately and told me about the fight. I rushed out of work so that we could get in the car and look for Ryan. We soon found him walking toward home with his head hanging low. Quickly, we checked him over. His clothes weren't ripped, he wasn't limping or holding his arm in pain, and there was no sign of bleeding or bruising. We were relieved.

As soon as he got in the car, it was clear that he'd been in a fight. His adrenaline was still so high that his hands were trembling.

"We got a call from Mr. Emory," I said. "Tell me what happened."

"Well, Dad, before he got there and broke it up, I got in a few good punches and I don't think Mason will ever bother me again."

I wasn't upset with Ryan. I was proud. "Way to go, buddy! Way to stick up for yourself and hold your ground. I hope you taught this kid a lesson today," I said.

For the rest of Ryan's seventh grade year, I checked in with him regularly. "Is everything alright? Has Mason bothered you since the fight in the park?"

"No, Dad, he hasn't bothered me a single bit. He still bullies other kids at school, but not me."

It didn't make me happy to hear that Mason was bullying other kids, but I was relieved to hear that the target was off Ryan's back. Then, one day, his answer to my "checking in" question stunned me. "You know what, Dad? I'm actually friends with him now. He's kind of cool. He's not such a bad guy." With widened eyes I said, "Ryan, you're kidding me! This kid has been on your case since the fifth grade. What makes you think you can trust him now?"

"People change. He's really okay now," claimed Ryan.

"Look, Ryan, I know some people can become better over time, but I'm not convinced he's changed that much."

Ryan looked at me and said, very seriously, "Dad, don't worry about it. Give me my space. I'm old enough to choose my own friends."

What could I have said to that?

Kelly and I agonized over what Ryan had told me and what he said about the new "friendship" between himself and Mason. We both thought it was a terrible decision. Mason's bullying was too relentless and too long-term to be a fluke. But, in the end, we agreed that at age thirteen, Ryan was old enough to make some decisions on his own. If this one turned out to be a bad one, as we suspected it would, then it would become a tough but necessary life lesson.

"We'll just be there if Ryan needs us," Kelly said.

"Or *when* he needs us," I added.

I felt like we were setting Ryan up for a fall by allowing him to talk to Mason. But, at the same time, we realized that sometimes kids need to learn things the hard way and on their own. Maybe Ryan needed to learn that you cannot trust everybody, even if they claimed to have changed.

I had no idea how much we would regret that decision in the years to come.

4

THE BIGGEST REGRET OF MY LIFE

THE START of Ryan's eighth-grade school year seemed to be more difficult academically than prior years. Homework was becoming a major source of distress. Schoolwork and homework were always a challenge for Ryan. He was a solid C student, but now something seemed different. He was doing worse than ever academically, and he lacked self-confidence and motivation.

"I'm just stupid! I can't do this!" Ryan would yell.

"You're not stupid," we would tell him. However, it was obvious that he had internalized a lot of the bullying that went on during seventh grade and it was having a negative impact on him and his school performance. The bully's voice had become *his* inner voice. On several occasions, he ended up in tears at the dinner table, convinced that he would not pass eighth grade.

"They're going to put me back in SPED," he'd say, crying. "I don't want to go back to that!"

The truth was that we didn't know if being identified

again was a real risk or not. Ryan was struggling academically, so it would not have been the end of the world if he ended up getting special education services again. However, Ryan was sure it would mean total social collapse for him amongst his peers.

On the evening of September 30, 2003, one week before Ryan's death, I came home from work and found Kelly and Ryan sitting at the kitchen table. His tearstained face made it obvious to me that he was very upset about something. Ryan had just told Kelly that school progress reports were coming out that Friday and he confessed that he was failing. As Kelly finished telling me what had just occurred, Ryan started to cry again and asked me if he could talk to me alone in my office downstairs. Kelly understood that Ryan and I had a special bond with one another. Therefore, he often preferred to confide in me, much the same way Megan preferred to speak with Kelly about her problems. So, with Kelly's encouragement, we headed downstairs to my office for a father-son talk. I was confident that I would be able to console Ryan and help him to feel better about his current situation, as this was usually the case.

As Ryan began speaking, I realized that he wanted to forewarn me that he was not just failing math – he was failing all of his other subjects too. Understanding how difficult this was for him I said, "I'm so proud of you for having the courage to come to us about your grades beforehand rather than wait until Friday when the reports come home. That took a lot of maturity on your part, buddy." However, Ryan kept crying and said, "I'm just a dumbass, so what's the use?" I couldn't believe he thought that about himself. It hurt me to hear him say that. After realizing how upset Ryan was, I told him that when I was his age, I was not a good student either. It was not because I was stupid, but because I wasn't able to focus. I told Ryan that I felt this might be his problem as well. I said, "You are definitely not a dumbass, Ryan – just very disorganized. Frankly, it seems like you are more interested in your computer than doing your homework lately." It was after this comment that Ryan asked me a question that will haunt me for the rest of my life. "Dad, when you were my age, did you ever feel like killing yourself?"

Suddenly, I had a flashback to my own teenage years. Like many teenagers, I was moody and emotional and took the opinions of others to heart. At times, I had feelings of self-doubt and a desire to fit in with the popular crowd. I, too, desperately wanted to be accepted by my peers. I often found myself rebelling against authority and feeling insecure about my own future. I knew I had to be honest with Ryan. I did not want him to feel as if he was the only person that ever felt the way he was feeling. As a teenager, there were definitely times when I thought about killing myself too.

I sat there facing my distraught son. Not only knowing but truly understanding his pain, I reluctantly said, "Yes. There were indeed times when I was close to your age that I thought suicide might be the only way to stop feeling emotional pain. Often it was when my heart was rejected by a girl that I liked." I explained to Ryan that this kind of pain in life was inevitable. There will always come a time when you love someone, but they don't love you back in the same way. Although it hurts, it will eventually get better. At that moment, he shot me a look through his tears. Looking back at that moment, I realized that the look he gave me resembled a fear of discovery. It was as if his eyes were saying, "Oh my God, you know about that?"

Regrettably, I quickly changed the topic from girls since it appeared that Ryan didn't want to go there and, instead, stressed to him all of the wonderful things I would have missed if I had killed myself. I explained to him that I would have never met his mother and fallen in love. I would have never had my three wonderful children, and I would have never experienced all the love and joy we had as a family.

In that moment, I felt what he needed was a good pep talk and a hug. However, I was only partially correct. Ryan was waving a red flag right in front of me and I did not see it. I did not believe that it was possible he could be truly feeling suicidal and did not for a moment believe that he would actually take his life. In hindsight, Ryan needed more help than I gave him.

Towards the end of our conversation, I reassured Ryan that I was not going to let him fail the eighth grade and that I would help him get back on track. We made a plan to do his homework in my office together so that I could always be available to help him. As we hugged, tears running down our faces, I said, "If you ever killed yourself, it would break my heart into a million pieces. Promise me you will never do it." He promised me that he wouldn't, and I believed him. He seemed calmer and I thought that he felt better.

As we hugged again, Ryan asked me to do something that ended up being the biggest regret of my life. He asked me not to tell his mother what he told me about killing himself. "She'll just make me go back to that counselor. It was a waste of time," he said. When he mentioned this, he was smiling again, and he seemed okay, so I assured him that our talk would be kept a secret between us.

After our conversation, he left my office seemingly happy and, quite honestly, I felt proud of myself that I was able to handle that difficult conversation so well. I believed that everything would be fine, and that Ryan would get through this difficult time with our support. I was confident that he knew I loved him unconditionally and that I was there for him any time he wanted to talk.

Little did I know, this couldn't have been further from the truth.

5

THE WORST DAY OF MY LIFE

OCTOBER 6, 2003, 6 p.m., LaGuardia Airport, NYC, United Terminal, Gate #2. This date, time, and place will forever be etched into my memory. It would end up being the last time I ever spoke to my son. I had just arrived in New York City from Burlington, Vermont for business. I was there to catch my connecting flight to Rochester, New York. There was time to check in with my wife, so I called home. We had our typical back and forth about our days. Nothing memorable came up. It was just the usual mundane stuff discussed between the two of us on an uneventful day. Then, I asked her to put Ryan on the phone. I wanted to know how his day went and how he was feeling. I was still a little concerned about his state of mind, especially related to school. Ryan did not let on that there was anything bothering him. He said he had a pretty good day at school. I reminded him that I would not be home until Thursday. Then I said, "I love you, Ryan." He replied, "I love you too, Dad." Those would be the last words between us. What was about to unfold over the next twelve hours was truly unstoppable destiny. I am so grateful those were our last words.

On the morning of October 7, I woke up to the sound of my cell phone ringing. I thought it was just the alarm I had set the night before. Why was it ringing now? I was still groggy from travelling the night before. My bleary eyes began to focus on the familiar number flashing on the caller ID. It was Kelly calling from home. I could not imagine why she would call me so early.

Kelly was crying and incoherently yelling something at first. I couldn't make out what she was saying, I was still waking up. I hopped out of bed and rubbed my eyes. "Oh my God, Johnny, you have to come home right away!" she then said more clearly in a hysterical voice.

"Why honey? What's wrong?" I asked.

"Ryan hanged himself! Come home now!"

Not believing the worst, I asked stupidly, "Oh my God, is he alright?"

"No, he's not alright" she screamed at me. "He's dead! He's dead!" She sobbed like I had never heard her do before.

I burst out in disbelief, "Oh my God, please no!" I heard the words but didn't believe what I was hearing. "He's dead?!" She repeated it and I questioned her again, with much more panic in my voice, "He's dead?" We volleyed like this a few more times and the horror began to sink deep into my soul. It was pain like I never felt before in my life. I couldn't breathe. I felt like someone had taken a sledgehammer to my chest. I snapped the cell phone closed and dropped it on the floor in horror. "This can't be real! I'm just having the worst nightmare! I need to wake up! Please God, wake me up!" I just stood there in shock and then the most all-consuming feeling of heartache came over me. I started to shake and fell to the ground and into a fetal position. "This can't be happening. My God, I just talked to him yesterday on the phone, he sounded so upbeat. He said he loved me. Why would he do this? Why!!!???"

I got up and just threw my jeans and sweater on that I wore the day before. I probably left some stuff in that room while I hastily packed. "Who cares?" I thought, I just had to get out of there. I entered the elevator and began to sob again. I leaned against the back wall of the elevator, holding my head in my hands, letting uninhibited wracking sobs come forward. At one point the elevator stopped at another floor on the way down. It was an elderly couple waiting to board; when they saw me, they recoiled back and let the doors close. I never felt so alone in my life, as I descended into a living hell that would continue to unfold for the rest of that day.

I made it out to my rental car and somehow found the strength and ability to drive to the airport. As I was driving all I could think about was poor Kelly and Megan dealing with this nightmare all by themselves. And poor Conor with his autism – he probably had no idea what hell had just unfolded upon his family. I just had to get to them as quickly as possible. What a nightmare that moment truly was. Maybe I should call my family, I thought. They could get to Kelly sooner from Long Island, but my mind could barely focus, much less remember a ten-digit number. Fortunately, I had called my sister Donna the night before, so the number was in the outgoing call log. I highlighted it and pressed the dial button. In between choking sobs, I said, "Donna, it's me! Ryan committed suicide! He hanged himself!" My sister, of course, responded with shocked disbelief. "I'm on my way back but it may take all day, will you please try to get to Kelly? She can't be alone. I'm begging you!" Donna agreed to do her best, and notify the rest of the family, including my mother. I had just lost my father six months earlier after a prolonged stay at a nursing home after suffering several strokes. I didn't think my mother would survive after hearing this news. "Oh, dear God, this will kill her," I thought to myself.

I got to the airport, hastily leaving my rental car still running with the Hertz attendant. No time to do the return paperwork. "I'm sorry, I have a family emergency and I just can't deal with this right now," is all I said to him. I ran into the terminal, dragging my suitcase, with my computer bag thrown over my shoulders. I must have looked completely disheveled since I didn't even bother to comb my hair or brush my teeth before I left the hotel room. I ran up to the United Airlines ticket counter, oblivious to the others still waiting in line. Sobbing, I blurted out to the ticket counter clerk, "My son committed suicide! Please get me on a flight as soon as possible back to Burlington, Vermont." I fumbled through my wallet with my hands shaking, trying to find the IBM-issued business credit card. The best the clerk could do was a flight leaving in an hour with a connection in Philadelphia. "Oh God, I won't be home until about two in the afternoon!" As he was processing my boarding pass, my head fell into my hands again. As I wiped my tearstained face, I could see the looks of pity among the others in line.

Now I had to get through security – another nightmare experience since this was post-9/11. Of course, I was considered a high risk since I just purchased my one-way ticket with a credit card and I was clearly unstable. They kept asking me to calm down and explain why I was in such a rush. Then, they made me put my arms out and patted me down as if I might have a weapon on me. I felt so humiliated as I kept crying out, "My son is dead. He killed himself. Please God, will you just let me through."

After finally getting on the plane, I sat down in my window seat and looked out to nothing but a blur because my eyes were so filled with tears. I kept asking myself over and over again, "Why?" He had seemed so upbeat yesterday on the phone and during our heart-to-heart conversation a few weeks ago over his lousy progress report – a conversation I had thought went so well. I thought Ryan was just as optimistic as I was that he would get his grades back on track. I was consumed with heartache and bewilderment. Ryan had two parents who loved him so much and a sister and brother who adored him too. He seemed to be well-liked and had a lot of friends. They were always calling for him. He seemed to be generally enjoying life. I knew Ryan had been down on himself about his grades recently, but this wasn't the first bad progress report he had gotten. I really thought I helped him put it all in perspective.

I don't really remember much about the connection in Philly. It must have been a quick layover. The whole morning, I ate nothing. Feeding myself was not even a thought. Though I don't remember exactly when, I called home to let Kelly know I was on my way. I do remember calling my manager and friend, Dave Balkin. He already knew about Ryan's death since his daughter was in Ryan's class and word travelled through Essex Junction that morning very quickly. He said he would pick me up at the airport in Burlington. My mind and heart rate kept racing. I thought for sure I was going to have a heart attack and the thought of dying at that point was not an unwanted one. "How will I ever survive this?" I remember thinking.

The plane began circling over the airport in Burlington. It was a beautiful day without any clouds to obstruct the view. I thought about how obscene it was that an unimaginable nightmare had descended upon my family on such a beautiful early autumn New England day. I got off the plane and walked over to the baggage claim area, where Dave met up with me. He hugged me and I just sobbed all over again. I remember at one point, while waiting for my luggage on the carousel, I fell to my knees. "This just can't be happening!" I kept crying out as Dave tried to console me. What a scene I must have created at the airport. I was oblivious to my surroundings at that point. Dave drove me home. I remember telling him how bad I felt for him to have to handle what was probably one of the worst-case personnel issues as a manager. I kept apologizing to him for having to deal with this. He kept saying, "Please stop, John, I'm your friend first. Don't be ridiculous."

The drive back to Essex Junction seemed to take forever. I remember seeing people on the street, in their cars, smiling or laughing and I just started to get so angry at the world. "How dare they be happy right now! How dare they! Damn all of you!" I'm sure I sounded like a crazy person to Dave, but he understood. As we finally pulled into the driveway, I could see Megan standing in the doorway, crying and hugging a neighbor who was trying to comfort her. I ran to her and hugged her and soon it was a threesome hug at the door entry as Kelly quickly joined us. For the three of us, our whole world was now shattered, and our only response was to grab onto one another like a life preserver, telling each other how much we loved each other over and over again.

Conor appeared, looking up at the three of us. Confused, he cried, "Please smile again, please smile again." He was only six years old, and his young age and his autism made it too difficult for him to comprehend what had happened that morning. He just wanted us all to stop crying and smile again. It was in that moment, I knew as the father, I needed to pull myself together for the sake of my family, but especially for Conor. He was now my only son. He needed his dad to be strong again. I'll confess, I had started that day wanting to kill myself too – the pain was just too much. But at that moment, the thought was erased by my sense of duty to be the strong one for my family.

I immediately asked Kelly where Ryan was. I wanted to see him for myself. I just couldn't believe it! Kelly said he was at the funeral home. They were going to do an autopsy first. She didn't think they would let me see him that day. Police Chief David Demag then appeared at our home. He heard I arrived home and he just wanted to comfort me. He shared with me his own loss of his son just that past February to a motorcycle accident in Las Vegas. He wanted me to know he understood this pain of losing a son and he was there to help me deal with my loss. I begged him to take me to the funeral home. He agreed, and Kelly came too.

When we arrived, the funeral director took us to a room downstairs, the place where they prepare the bodies for the wake and funeral. Kelly and I walked into the room and there lay my son's body on a simple long metal table, covered with a white sheet. They pulled it down just enough to show his head. He looked so peaceful. I kissed Ryan's cold forehead. I pressed my head against his and cried, just like we had done together only one week earlier. This will forever be the worst day of my life.

6

THE AFTERMATH AND WHAT REALLY HAPPENED

A FEW DAYS after Ryan's funeral, I found myself in his room, sitting at the desk where my beloved son did his homework and used his computer. I cried so hard, "Please God, give me a second chance to do it all right. I would do anything for a do-over." I looked up at the shelf I had installed for him a few years ago to hold books and memorabilia. There, staring me right in the face, was Ryan's yearbook from seventh grade. I took it down and started to turn the pages. I just wanted to find his picture and touch it.

As I got to the seventh-grade section, I noticed something disturbing. Some of the photos of students had been drawn on, scribbled out, and there were angry comments written by Ryan. When I got to the photo of Mason, the bully, I discovered that Ryan had written so much over his face that the page had ripped from the excessive pressure of his pen. He was not only mad at Mason, and others, but surprisingly at a girl in his class too. Interestingly, he drew stars around his friends and even a crown on the head of a particularly close friend. I suddenly felt Ryan's presence, like he was trying to send me a message. All I could hear in my head over and over again was, "Dad, something went terribly wrong at school."

At this point, I turned on Ryan's computer, thinking maybe he left a note on it. I thought perhaps his AIM (AOL Instant Messenger) program might have some clues since he spent most of his time on it. I typed in Ryan's screen name and then typed in the password. I knew it because we had a family rule that the password was shared with me in case something happened to him. As most parents were back then, I was mostly worried about predators and pedophiles. As I would discover, the bigger threat was one I had never anticipated: cyber-bullying.

Instantly Ryan was back online, and it startled his classmates on his buddy list. Chat windows suddenly popped up. "Who is this?" "What are you doing?" "This isn't funny!" "Get off of Ryan's account!" I replied to every one of them, "I'm Ryan's dad. I'm just trying to find out what happened. Does anyone here know why Ryan did what he did?"

The mystery started to unravel rapidly. A few windows popped up, and a few classmates began to tell me what happened between Ryan and Mason. One particular young lady started off, "Mr. Halligan, you need to know this probably had nothing to do with you or your wife. Some things happened at school that Ryan may not have told you about." She went on to tell me that Ryan had told Mason a story towards the end of seventh grade about a medical exam he had a few months prior.

At some point during the school year, Ryan had developed a severe bout of constipation and abdominal pain. Kelly took him to his doctor. During this evaluation, the doctor performed a DRE (digital rectal examination) as part of the assessment and determination of the severity of his constipation. Ryan's situation was assessed and treated. His illness soon after was resolved. Fast forward a few months later, Ryan thought the DRE was something funny to share with his new "friend," Mason. Well, Mason turned this into a rumor that Ryan was gay because he claimed Ryan said he liked it. This young lady I was now chatting with went on to explain how many of Ryan's classmates started to tease him about the rumor. Ryan would often hide in the boys' bathroom to avoid people in between classes. She said he was often seen visibly upset during the school day. She believed this was what drove Ryan to kill himself.

As the night went on, even more was revealed to me. Another student suggested I might find something more on Ryan's computer. He went on to explain that many of the middle schoolers were using a freeware program called DeadAIM, which was an add-on program that allowed the user to manage multiple screen names more easily. Students would have various screen names and often pretend to be different people. This was something they thought was fun to do. They often tried to impersonate each other as well. Another feature of this add-on was the option to easily save all past chats in a folder on a computer's hard drive. Well, sure enough, this was what I found on Ryan's computer.

In the "My Documents" folder, I first found a folder titled "AIM LOGS." In that folder I noticed what appeared to be hundreds of folders titled by individual screen names. Inside those folders, I found actual conversations Ryan had with that screen name. There was so much to read. And as I read these conversations, my heart began to break all over again. I finally discovered why he was on his computer so much that last summer. He was trying to deal with the rumor that was spread that he was gay. During that same time, it was also evident that he approached a female classmate online and had shared some very personal feelings and thoughts with her. They continued to chat for most of the summer, but those conversations appeared to end rather abruptly in September, at the start of his eighth grade school year.

Shortly after the discovery of these chat messages, the detective working on Ryan's case came to our home to share his findings. He, too, had a copy of Ryan's hard drive and was doing the same kind of searches I had performed and also came across the AIM logs. He also had interviewed the students, including Ryan's friends, to gather more information. I shared with him what I found in his yearbook. One critical piece of information the detective shared with us was something Ryan said to a fellow student on the last day of his life. Ryan went up to a girl and said, "It's girls like you who make me want to kill myself." The detective gave me the name of the girl, and it was the same girl on whose yearbook picture Ryan had written angry comments. Of course, this got our attention and so we had even more questions. Why would Ryan say such a thing and why was he so angry with this person?

Kelly and I asked Ryan's friends to meet with us the next day after school. We sat down together and shared what we knew at that point. We pleaded with them to share any more information. They began to open up more and shared that Ryan had a crush on a girl, named Ainsley, all summer long. (This name has been changed, as discussed in the Author's Note at the beginning of the book.) She was going to be his first girlfriend. However, they found out after Ainsley rejected him in person, that she and her friends thought it would be funny for her to pretend to like him online. Ainsley shared the private conversations between her and Ryan with her friends as proof that she was succeeding in fooling him during the summer. When the new school year started, Ryan approached her while she was standing with her friends in the courtyard, thinking everything was great between them. In a snobby tone, Ainsley humiliated Ryan telling him that he was "a loser" and that she never liked him. She and her friends then laughed and walked away. Ryan fought back the tears as he tried to pretend he didn't care in front of his friends. He didn't talk about it, but one of his friends could sense he was hurting. Ryan's friends said he was not the typical happy-go-lucky kid they knew throughout grade school. Ryan became darker in his personality, demeanor, and conversations.

Ryan's friends explained to us that he began bringing up stories at the lunch table about kids who committed suicide. In particular, he mentioned a high school boy in our community who had just taken his own life that summer. His friends got into the topic too, just thinking it was cool to talk about it in a macabre way. They never thought Ryan would commit suicide. Tragically, these teenagers were not educated about the warning signs and the urgent need to let an adult know when a friend becomes preoccupied with this topic.

In addition to the cyberbullying text messages I found on Ryan's computer, I also uncovered a very unhealthy online relationship with another boy. The two of them spent much time during September and up to the day Ryan died commiserating about how "life sucks." They shared websites of gruesome death scenes and suicides. They also found an online questionnaire which helps you determine if you should kill yourself. The boys laughed that they both got the same answer, results indicating that they should kill themselves. They also shared websites with one another about different methods to commit suicide. The last exchange, and most disturbing, I found between them was the following:

Ryan: Tonight is the night I'm going to kill myself!

Other Boy: It's about %$#@ing time!

7

THE HEALING POWER OF FORGIVENESS

SHORTLY AFTER UNCOVERING what happened between Ryan and Ainsley, we were told that word had gotten out about what happened between them. Many classmates were now harassing Ainsley at school and online for what they believed – that she had caused Ryan to commit suicide. It was getting so intense that she was trying to avoid school. Ainsley's friends were now concerned about her mental health and potentially suicidal response to the situation. When I heard of this, I became heartsick. The last thing Kelly and I wanted was for another family to lose a child to suicide.

I'm not even sure why at this time I already had an instinctive feeling that Ryan's suicide was more than just an impulsive response to being rejected by Ainsley. I had been rejected by a girl when I was in seventh grade, but not once had suicidal thoughts entered my mind at that age. I do recall having these feelings later on in high school, but that was after breaking up with a girl after several months of dating. Ryan had not even met up with Ainsley for one date. Like Ryan, when I was in seventh grade I had expressed an interest, through mutual friends, in a girl who was a grade older than me. I heard she liked me too. There was even a moment at a school dance when we awkwardly swayed to a song. But days later she said my hair was too short and she didn't like me anymore because of the awful haircut my parents forced on me. (This was the seventies, when crew cuts were not cool.) Stupid, shallow, but typical mean middle school behavior is all that was in retrospect. In Ryan's case, perhaps the sharing of personal chat conversations was a bit more, but there is no way I could be convinced that this was the sole reason why he killed himself. What about all the bullying that went on since fifth grade? I believed that had the effect of chipping away at his self-esteem and perhaps made him more vulnerable when Ainsley rejected him.

To blame Ryan's death entirely on Ainsley would have been dishonest and unfair. The reasons for suicide are much more complicated, in my opinion. I believe, in the end, Ryan had some level of depression which may have been caused by environmental or a brain chemistry imbalance, or maybe a combination of both. We'll never know for sure since we never had him formally diagnosed or assessed for depression. But again, there was no way this could all be pinned on Ainsley. It would have been convenient to blame this all on one person, but it just felt very unfair to do this to a thirteen-year-old girl. I also had evidence on his computer and through his chats with others that he was thinking of suicide well before he found out that Ainsley did not really like him. So I knew this was not just about her, and perhaps not really about her at all. Yes, one could argue that maybe she was the one to push him over the edge. But again, there was no way I could be convinced this was all her fault.

Immediately after learning of the harassment of Ainsley by her classmates, I called her home and spoke to her mother. Her mother was so grateful for the call and was very apologetic. Ainsley's mother was ashamed of her daughter's behavior, but she was also terrified of what she might do to herself. I asked if it would be alright for both of them to come to our home for a conversation. I was grateful when she accepted the invitation.

It was not long after we hung up that the doorbell rang. I opened the door and hugged them both as they stepped in. Ainsley then hugged me so tightly again, I could feel her nervousness. I also could feel her sorrow and regret. For most of the visit, she said very little since she was so choked up. I believe it took overwhelming courage for her to even come to our home. I immediately felt sadness and compassion for this young lady. We sat down on the couch in the front room of our house. As I sat next to Ainsley, I took her hand and with a low tone of voice, I said, "Ainsley, you did a mean thing. But I don't believe you are a mean person. I don't believe for a second that you would have done what you did if you knew Ryan was going to do what he did. This is not your fault. Ryan had other problems that I believe were much more significant factors than what happened between the both of you. This is not your fault." We hugged and cried together for a little while longer. Her mother went on to share with us that her own adult brother, Ainsley's uncle, had died by suicide just a few months earlier. She shared how hard it had been for her family, especially for her parents. She was so heartsick to have this connection to Ryan now too. She suggested we join them for a Survivors of Suicide support group that met monthly in Burlington, Vermont. I was grateful for the suggestion. I could sense Ainsley was drained emotionally but seemed to have a huge weight taken off her shoulders. That was all I wanted to accomplish, so we hugged again, and I thanked them both for giving me the opportunity to clear the air with them.

After they left, I called a few parents of Ryan's friends to let them know we met with Ainsley and that Ryan's suicide was not her fault. I asked them to please have their sons defend Ainsley and get the word out that the Halligans did not feel she was in any way responsible for Ryan's death. Apparently, this was successful because we later heard that the kids were leaving Ainsley alone and that she appeared to be doing much better.

As for the bully, quite honestly, I wanted to kill this kid for all the heartache he brought upon Ryan and then our family too. If it were not for Kelly's more rational, calm response in keeping me in check, I would probably be writing this book from prison right now. As part of my own attempt to deflect my anger, I began to pursue a bullying prevention law in memory of Ryan. In the meantime, I was just doing my best to focus my pain onto a more productive path.

However, just a few weeks into December, I received a phone call from a father of one of Ryan's friends. His voice was very nervous and shaky as he began to say, "John, this is a tough call for me to make. When I got home from work this evening, I found my son very upset. I asked him why and, at first, I had a hard time believing him." He went on to tell me, "My son said that Mason and others in his group of friends are saying things like, Ryan was weak. He couldn't handle life. And that he was gay."

When I received this phone call, Kelly wasn't home. I grabbed my keys and my coat, and I headed out the door. I reverted to my earlier feelings of rage. I wanted to kill this kid. But, thank God, I was slowed down enough to allow my initial anger to diffuse a bit. There is a very infamous traffic light, an intersection in the center of Essex Junction called "Five Corners." At this intersection five roads come together rather than just four. This traffic light is a nightmare. If you don't get to this intersection at a green light, you end up waiting a very long time as the green light rotates through every entering road and left turn lane.

As I pulled up to the light, it had just changed from yellow to red. I sat there for what felt like forever, gripping the steering wheel so hard. I kept imagining in my mind the perfect scene when I arrived at this kid's home: Light changes. I get to his home. Knock on the door. Hopefully, he answers! Grab him by the shirt. Pull him out into the front yard. And just beat the heck out of him!

Sure enough, my wife's voice popped into my head. When the light finally changed, I had a different plan. I got to Mason's house and knocked on the door. Sure enough... he answered. He had no idea who I was. We had never met in person before. He didn't go to Ryan's wake or funeral. But I knew who he was because Ryan pointed him out to me several times. I took a deep breath and asked him, "Is your mom or dad home?"

He replied, "Yes."

"Can I please speak to one of them?"

The mother came to the front door, and I introduced myself to her. She quickly recognized my name and went on about how sorry she was for our loss.

I said, "Well, I appreciate that. But can I please come into your home? I need to speak to you about something."

She invited me inside, and we went into the living room. The boy's father was there watching TV; he clicked it off. As we were about to sit down, I realized their son was not there, so I asked her, "Can you please get your son? He needs to come in here. He needs to hear what I have to say."

She got her son and introduced him to me. Now he knew I was Mr. Halligan. This kid looked like he was about to faint, and unfortunately for him, the only place to sit down was on the couch next to me.

We sat down, and I turned to him and said, "You probably have no idea. You probably have no idea, the amount of pain you created in my son's life. So much pain because of you and your friends who decided to bully my son, since the fifth grade, about the two issues he struggled with for most of his life. And I just received this phone call tonight, and I'm finding out that you are continuing to bully my son. My son who is no longer here to even defend himself."

I then went on to describe the words he was now saying about Ryan at the middle school. At this point, he went into complete denial. "Oh, Mr. Halligan, I would never say such a thing. I liked your son. He was a cool kid."

Never taking my eyes off of him, I said, "You're lying to me. You're lying to me and you're lying to your parents right now. But you know what? I refuse to believe that you are that heartless, I refuse to believe that you are that empty of a soul. I think you are just a dumbass thirteen-year-old, trying to act tough, trying to keep this stupid bully reputation going on at the middle school. But I refuse to believe that you are this heartless."

An amazing thing happened next. This kid, this tough bully kid, started to cry. A tear rolled down his face. He began to sob. Over and over again he said, "I'm sorry, Mr. Halligan. I'm sorry. I'm sorry. I promise I'll never say another thing about Ryan. I'm sorry."

My wife and I always fantasize about somebody inventing a time machine – a machine we could step into, turn the clock back, and get a do-over here. Get to do anything different to keep my son alive. The harsh reality is that you cannot turn back time. There is no time machine. Time continues to march forward. Ryan is gone forever. But I have to tell you, at this particular point in time, hearing Mason say he was sorry, in a heartfelt, sincere way, meant a great deal to me. It meant a lot. I looked at his mom and dad. They were in stunned silence. I thought to myself, now is probably a good time to leave. I let myself out of the house, got in my car, and the whole way home I kept banging the steering wheel, overwhelmed with deep regret. "Why didn't I do this a lot sooner? Why didn't I knock on this kid's door back in the fifth grade and reach him the way I had reached him tonight?

I'm often asked, whatever became of Mason and Ainsley. As for Mason, I really don't know. I did not make it my mission to track him through life. It was a like a hot flame I did not want to touch again. But I have no doubt this story will stay with him for the rest of his life. And if by faith, I ever do see him again, I hope that he became a better person from this experience. I pray that if he became a parent, that he would be a better parent from this too. My wife and I do not wish him any ill. You may be surprised to hear this, but we don't. Kelly and I hold onto the faith that Ryan is with God, and we will see him again. And we both believe in forgiveness too. When the bully broke down and apologized, I knew that was an opportunity and I grabbed it. I held hate and revenge in my heart for two months and it nearly killed me. Forgiveness is a better state of mind. We both hold onto the faith that this kid eventually grew up. And that is good enough for us.

Ainsley turned out to be a very courageous young lady. In 2006, when she was a tenth grader, she agreed to appear with me on a national TV program. Ainsley took some very tough questions during the interview. She did it because she wanted to help. She wanted to in some way make up for her part in Ryan's story. Ainsley recognizes that her generation and the ones after hers now have the ability to hide behind a screen and say and do things one would not normally say or do in person. And because of this ability, there is now so much emotional abuse among young people that it has reached epidemic levels. Ainsley wishes she could step into a time machine too and take back everything she did that summer of 2003. But she can't, and we forgive her. I pray she has learned to forgive herself.

After many years of lost contact with Ainsley, I received a beautiful email from her in May 2017. In that email she reflected on the difficulties of her adolescent years, and the fact that her generation was the first to wrestle with the added pressure of online communications and social media during those years. She had, she wrote, learned a lot about compassion in the years since Ryan's death and was now much more aware of how her reactions affected others.

We agreed to meet for lunch that spring and we had

a wonderful conversation. Ainsley has grown to be a beautiful, sweet, and intelligent young woman. But to this day, she struggles with what happened back in middle school when she and her peers were so immature. Once again, I reminded her that we forgive her and that she needs to forgive herself. I pray that she does find her way.

8

LESSONS LEARNED

AFTER RYAN'S DEATH, I soon realized I had completely underestimated the effects the emotional bullying had on Ryan. I made the mistake of viewing my son's situation through my own childhood experiences. Perhaps you can relate to this too. Back in the seventh grade I had an issue with a particular boy. He physically intimidated me at times and I felt the social peer pressure to stand up to him to make it stop. We had a big fight after school one day, and that was the end of it. We avoided each other for the rest of our lives. We did not have the internet to come home to and torment each other all over again. This world in which our children are growing up is a very different one than most of us grew up in. This became so clear to me one day when a high school student came up to me after one of my presentations. He said, "You know, Mr. Halligan, I would actually prefer to get a black eye than have somebody spread rumors about me online. Because I can go to the adults, show them my black eye, and get a response. But it is almost impossible for me to show them my bruised heart."

These new forms of cyberbullying may be one reason that suicide is on the rise. The statistics are startling. Suicide is the third leading cause of death among youngsters. According to the Centers for Disease Control and Prevention, this results in about 4,600 deaths per year. The suicide rate for ten- to fourteen-year-olds has grown more than 50 percent over the last three decades.[1] The correlation between victims of bullying and suicide is staggering. Studies performed by researchers at Yale University show that victims of bullying are two to nine times more likely to consider suicide than those who are not bullied.[2] Megan Meier, Tyler Long, Ty Smalley, Phoebe Prince, Jamie Hubley, Ashawnty Davis, and Mallory Grossman are just a few who suffered this fate.

This leads me to some key lessons I have learned over the years.

The first lesson is that openly discussing suicide with your child will *not* increase the risk of them attempting suicide. I *now* know that what Ryan needed was for me to take a deep breath, swallow hard, and ask a set of critical questions. I should have said, "It sounds like you are thinking of suicide. Do you have a plan for how to end your life?" Yes, this is scary and difficult, but if you sense your child is starting to drift down this path, you need to stop and ask these questions. Be careful to not ask them with a judgmental or accusatory tone. Also, do not say, "You wouldn't do that, would you?" or "You wouldn't do something crazy, would you?" If you phrase it in this way or with an insensitive or judgmental tone, your child will close up and deny what he or she is truly feeling. And this could end up being a very tragic mistake on your part. This is one thing I wrestle with still to this day. Ryan waved a big red flag in my face, and I mishandled the warning signs.

Statistics show that those who attempt suicide give warning signs. It is important to be familiar with these red flags.

- Talking or joking about suicide
- Talking about being a burden to others
- Drawing or writing about death
- Making statements about feeling worthless, hopeless, or helpless
- Isolating and withdrawing from family and friends
- Researching ways to die on the internet
- Changes in appearance, hygiene, eating, sleeping
- Changes in grades or quality of schoolwork
- Depression, loss of interest in the things one cares about
- Displaying mood swings
- Expressing rage and/or anger

- Dramatic changes in personality, acting out of character, becoming rebellious, engaging in self-destructive or risk-taking behaviors
- Getting in touch with loved ones, texting goodbyes
- Giving possessions away
- Use or increased use of alcohol or drugs

If your child is having thoughts of suicide, it is imperative to get help immediately. There are a number of great resources to connect with. Heading straight to the emergency department of your local hospital or calling 911 are immediate options if your child is at imminent risk. There are suicide and mental health hotlines that can also be called for assistance. The national suicide prevention website is https://suicidepreventionlifeline.org/ and the hotline is **1-800-273-8255**. Also available is the 211 dialing code for community information and referral services. This great resource offers many referral services for mental health and health resources, including counseling, support groups, drug and alcohol treatment, health insurance programs, clinics, and hospitals. In some states, such as Connecticut, 211 also offers Mobile Crisis Intervention Services. A trained mental health professional can immediately assist and assess your child who is experiencing a behavioral or mental health crisis. The crisis counselor may intervene by phone or in person at your home.

One of the startling discoveries highlighted in Ryan's autopsy report was evidence of wrist cutting. We were not aware. I recalled that Ryan and some of his friends were often wearing leather wrist bands. Young people who cut typically hide the marks with wrist bands or they wear long sleeve shirts. Sometimes they will cut somewhere else, like inner thighs, ankles, or anywhere that can be easily concealed.

The number of teens engaging in self-injurious behaviors is on the rise. The behavior of intentionally harming oneself is also known as cutting or self-mutilation. The most common form of this is cutting, but can also include burning, scratching, hair pulling, and punching oneself. There is a significant difference between suicide and self-harm and that is the intent. Many teens who engage in self-harming behaviors believe it is a way to cope with life; they may not be suicidal. The pain or sight of blood reassures them that they are still alive. Those who are suicidal have a deep sense of despair and see no other way out of the pain that they are experiencing in life. Self-harm and suicide are not always linked together, but in Ryan's case they were. Therefore, it is also important to be aware of this behavior and ask if they are purposely harming themselves. Check your child's arms or legs for cuts. Be aware if your child is always wearing long sleeves, despite the weather, or making excuses for marks on his body. In addition, if you are finding scissors, knives, or razors in odd places, such as the nightstand, it is time to have a serious conversation with your child.

The second lesson I learned is that your child will not always tell you everything. I learned this lesson the hard way. In addition to the material and information I uncovered on Ryan's computer, I was crestfallen about the fact that he never told Kelly or me what was going on. I thought we had a very close relationship. I thought he always felt comfortable coming to me with any problem. I spent a lot of time on this issue in therapy until, one day, the therapist asked me, "When you were his age, did you tell your parents about every one of your mistakes or painful moments?" It didn't take me long to answer, "No." Ah, of course, most teenagers don't tell their parents everything. Part of adolescence is wanting to break away from mom and dad and feeling you can problem-solve on your own or with the help of your peers. At times, I did not want to disappoint my own parents or burden them with something when they already had the stress of working, paying bills, and just trying to manage the everyday life of a family. However, there were times in my young life where it would have been great and often a lot easier if I had another adult in my life besides my parents who I could confide in for help and advice.

I think it is crucial for parents to take the time to sit with their child and ask them this straightforward, yet essential question, "If something went wrong in your life, and you were too afraid to tell us, who would you tell instead?" If they don't have an answer to that question, help them find one. This "go-to" person could be a school counselor, social worker, favorite teacher, family friend, neighbor, or relative. It is essential to help your child develop these connections and encourage them to trust these relationships. In doing so, they will feel more comfortable seeking out adult support, especially in a crisis.

As a parent, you need to let go of the notion that your child should always and only confide in you. Don't fool yourself into believing that just because you feel you have a beautiful, close relationship with your child, that you don't need this option. You do not want your child to solely depend on friends because they lack the vast experience of life and do not have the wisdom of time and perspective. So, get a "go-to" adult for your child in place!

The third lesson that I learned is that children should *not* have unrestricted and unmonitored use of technology. The conventional wisdom, back when Ryan was alive, was to remove computers from children's bedrooms and only allow use in a highly trafficked family area location. Back in this period, most parents were worried about pedophiles and predators. There were horrible stories in the media of young people meeting up with a stranger they first met online and then being kidnapped, sexually assaulted, and perhaps even killed. That conventional wisdom became obsolete with the introduction of the smartphone. Therefore, my family had the "no strangers" rules in place.

- No chatting with strangers online

- No sharing of personal information with a stranger online
- No sending a picture of yourself to a stranger online

In addition to the no stranger rules, we had another important safety rule: no secret passwords. I told my children, "You have to give me all of your account screen names and I will make up one password for you to use for all of these accounts. I promise you I will not use it to spy on you or read your personal stuff. But, God forbid, if you disappear one day, I do not want to waste any precious time trying to get lawyers or law enforcement to help me gain access to your accounts. Time will be critical. I will want to get in there as soon as possible to see what you did last online and who you communicated with last."

I thought I had it all covered until I reflected upon what I had discovered on Ryan's computer. It never crossed my mind that his peers could be just as harmful as a stranger online. As a parent, I had believed Ryan's computer use was a productive tool in helping him become a better student. I did not foresee how intense and addictive the social media use would be to Ryan and his peers. I was not aware of the potential pitfalls for Ryan in navigating cyberspace before he was mature enough to handle what he would encounter there. Although this was right before Myspace and well before Facebook, AOL Instant Messenger gave us a precursor of what was going to be the next craze for teens. The addictive draw to be online and continuously connected to your friends well into the evening was already taking root. A whole new set of concerns and rules were needed well before most parents even realized it. For us, this realization was tragically too late.

So often I am asked, "What is the appropriate age for a child to have a smartphone?" I often refer to the answer given by Tom Kersting, author of *Disconnected: How to Reconnect Our Digitally Distracted Kids*. This therapist and middle school counselor often replies, "When you are comfortable with your child having easy access to hardcore pornography." The truth is the internet is a gateway to this material which is inappropriate for children. It only takes a single exposure and their childhood innocence ends abruptly. Due to the ease of access, many teens have become addicted to pornography. It is the job of parents to protect their youngsters from this type of material. Unlimited access to the internet is dangerous.

So often parents believe their child *needs* a smartphone for various reasons. One of the most common explanations I hear is that parents believe it is necessary for their child to have a smartphone to assist with physical safety, in case of an emergency. Unfortunately, parents may not be considering the psychological and emotional harm that comes along with social media. A basic phone, with no access to apps or camera technology, can be provided to a child to enhance physical safety. This offers the child an opportunity to learn responsibility with a basic phone to prepare them for the next level of access to a smart phone. Another common reason that parents often explain for premature smartphone use is they are concerned that the child will be left out by his or her peers. A great campaign to be aware of to combat this parenting pressure is Wait until 8th (http://www.waituntil8th.org/). "The Wait Until 8th pledge empowers parents to rally together to delay giving children a smartphone until at least 8th grade. By banding together, this will decrease the pressure felt by kids and parents alike over the kids having a smartphone."

Once your child has met the appropriate age to have a smartphone, I encourage you to consider the following recommendations:

Website and App Inventory

- Ask your child to show you the sites he/she frequently visits and show you what he/she does. Three types of sites children commonly utilize are: instant or text messaging, social media, and video and picture posting.
- Open up accounts where your child has accounts, so you become familiar with how these apps are being used.
- If your child is under thirteen, you do have the option to have these accounts deleted. Most social media apps have an age requirement of thirteen and older in their

terms of use as mandated by the Federal Children's Online Privacy Protection Act of 1998.

- Have your child share with you all their user account names and passwords.
- Make certain your child never has and never will share his/her passwords with anyone, even a friend. Explain the risk of someone impersonating him/her and ruining their reputation.
- Have your child show you what he/she has in their profiles and pages. How does your child describe himself or herself? Is it all accurate and appropriate? Does it show too much detail about your child? Is your child protecting and sustaining a positive reputation? Are adequate privacy settings enabled?
- Scrutinize your child's friend lists on all social media accounts. Recognizing the identity of each person is paramount. If your child doesn't know the person in person, then consider that person a stranger. Request your child delete and block that person.

How to Discuss Bullying, Sexting, and Privacy

- Ask your child if he/she has ever been ridiculed, intimidated, or humiliated on the internet. Encourage your child to come to you for support if he/she is being bullied. Both of you should learn how to use the print screen or screen capture option to save evidence of the cyberbullying.

- In general, whether your child was bullied online or in person, write down the details as soon as possible. Log date, time, place, bully, bystanders, description of the event, and evidence. Bring this documentation to the appropriate school official or local police department, depending on the severity of the event.

- Ask whether your child has bullied anyone. It's important for him or her to appreciate how much unkind words or images can inflict emotional pain, and understand that the reach of the internet makes it far more destructive. Use Ryan's Story to make this point.

- Also, explain that this is a particularly difficult emotional period for many children and what may seem to be harmless teasing, can be devastating to the person being teased.

- Share with your child that the internet is a public forum, so anything can be shared with other people without their knowledge or consent. Emphasize the importance of being discreet in what your child says and does online. Your child needs to be vigilant in protecting his/her reputation. Things said and done on the internet can come back to haunt your child many years later.

- Have a very pointed conversation about "sexting," the risky practice of requesting and or sending sexually explicit photos or messages. Emphasize the point that these photos and messages can easily be forwarded on to others and damage his or her reputation. In addition, stress that it is against the law.

Family Technology Policy

- Establish clear and enforceable guidelines regarding internet and social media use.
- Create your family policy for acceptable technology use. List what may or may not be allowed, including clear rules about time limits.
- Be upfront with your child that this policy will be enforced and monitored. Try to set a policy that respects your child's privacy while also considering their age, maturity level, and inclination towards risky behavior.
- Purchase monitoring and time control software to help enforce your family's policy. Search "parental control software

reviews" to find the latest products, features, and reviews.

- Remove the technology (cells phones, tablets, iPods, computers) from the bedroom, specifically, when it is time to sleep.

Questions for Evaluating Your Child's Technology Use

Lastly, keep asking yourself the following questions as your child heads towards and moves through their adolescent years.

- How much technology and access does your child truly need? Take a minimalist approach to reduce the probability of addiction and stunted social skills.
- Does a middle school child or younger possess the maturity, judgment, and social skills to use text messaging and social websites responsibly? Do their peers?
- Does your child need a cell phone, particularly with text messaging and photo/video features? Is your child mature enough to handle these options responsibly? Would a very basic phone suffice until he or she is more mature?
- When does too much technology begin to hurt a child? Find the right balance with technology and with other activities.

- Is it healthy for your child to come home and plug right into their social network versus having some quiet, reflective, and regenerative time with the family?

Please refer to the resources section at the end of the book for more information.

9

DON'T BE A BYSTANDER, BE AN UPSTANDER

I FIRST WANT to be very clear that Ryan was not isolated or alone during his middle school years. He had some terrific friends. It did seem that he often hung out with the other kids that were also picked on. Ryan did have one friend, Raphael, who was so exceptional that Ryan drew a crown on top of his head in his seventh grade yearbook. Raphael was there to back him up for the fight with Mason. But how do you help your friend when a girl pretends to like them online and then tells them they were just kidding? How do you help your friend when others are spreading rumors that they are gay? There is only so much you can do as a young teen for your friend. Yes, you can listen to and support your friend emotionally. Ideally, they should tell an adult, but so often teens are resistant to going to adults for help. And it is usually moments like these that create a friend for life. I have no doubt Ryan and Raphael would have been lifelong friends.

Friends have power and bullies have power, but there is another group that has just as much power as either of these groups: bystanders. A bystander is one that just stands there and possibly laughs, which encourages the bully or, just as bad, decides to do nothing at all. Not intervene. Not stop it. I remember middle school and high school. I remember the kids who bullied usually did it for an audience. This is where the power comes from, and this is where the permission to bully comes from. If we start to chip away at the audience, we'll start to chip away the incentive to bully.

Had just one of Ainsley's friends that last summer said to her, "You have to stop. This isn't funny. You would not like it if a boy did it to you. If you did this to my brother, I would be so angry at you. You gotta stop. It isn't funny!" Had just one her friends had the strength and courage, Ainsley would have listened to them much more quickly than anyone else. And this could have been a completely different story. Had just one of Mason's friends said to him, "Stop calling Ryan gay. This is really not that funny. If you don't like Ryan, just leave him alone. Whether he is truly gay or not should matter anyway. Come on, just leave him alone." Had just one his friends had the strength and courage, Mason would have listened to them much more quickly than anyone else. And this could have been a completely different story. I remember the intensity of peer pressure at that age. We all cared far more what our peers thought of us than what the adults thought. That peer pressure can be such a dominant force in stopping bullying if we could just get them to push it in the right direction.

I can't stress the point enough – the students hold the power. They own the solution to this problem. Especially those who are friends of people who bully other people. They have the most power and the most influence over their friends. They are in the best position. I'm not asking them to tell on their friend or humiliate their friend in front of others. I, instead, give the simple advice to pull their friend aside during a private moment and just let them know how they feel – that it makes them feel uncomfortable and sad when their friend bullies others and that they want them to stop. If this is too hard to do in person, encourage your child to take advantage of technology and send a text message instead. I know this would still require a lot of courage, but this is the most powerful thing your child could do in a situation like this one. This could indeed be saving a life. So, as a parent, talk to your child about the role of bystanders and your expectations of your child to do the right thing.

Now I know in this conversation it may be common for your child to push back with the argument that "my *friend* may start to bully me instead." Well, if they do, my suggested answer is, "You just learned a very valuable lesson about this friendship. They are not a real friend. Make yourself a new friend because a real friend would appreciate your honesty. A real friend would appreciate you wanting them to be a better person." So I would beg them, "Don't be a bystander, be an upstander!" One friend of Ainsley, one friend of Mason, could have made Ryan's story a completely different one.

10

THEY WERE SENSITIVE TOO

I CAN'T TELL you how many times I have struck up a conversation with a stranger next to me in the airport or on a plane which leads to a discussion about suicide. So often while I'm travelling, I am asked what I do for a living. In almost all of these conversations, others have their own tragic story to tell – sometimes it's one of a lost friend, nephew, sibling, or even their child. Unfortunately, there are many survivors of suicide among us, quietly going along with their tremendous personal loss until they encounter someone whom they feel safe opening up to. Most of us feel safe with other survivors of suicide. Many, like me, think that discussing what happened eases our pain with a sense of purpose, which is to educate and prevent someone else from having this horrific experience. I am so grateful when someone does open up to me about their loss to suicide because I gain so much knowledge I can direct towards my prevention efforts.

For the past fifteen years, I have been a strong advocate for bullying and suicide prevention. Over these past years, so many parents have contacted me with their personal and family struggles with bullying and suicide. The saddest ones are from those who have just lost a child to suicide and soon after stumbled upon Ryan's website, in search of answers. I fully understand the desperation to find the answer to the question *Why?*. I always give these grieving souls as much time as they need to describe their own child's circumstances that led up to the suicide. Then, I ask them to please explain their child to me. The one common personality trait I hear over and over again is that their child was very sensitive. Perhaps, at times, they were highly sensitive. Typically, they often had a very emotional response to setbacks and hurt. While another child might have just shrugged it off, their child took things very personally. I have heard this described in every case I have encountered, and honestly, I have lost track of how many times I've heard it. I have even spoken to many parents in the high-profile cases, like my son's, and I heard the same description – their child was highly sensitive. I believe this is a critical personality trait we need to pay much more attention to when it comes to suicide prevention.

So, what is a highly sensitive child? Dr. Elaine Aron, expert on the highly sensitive child (HSC), describes this child as one who is "born with a nervous system that is highly aware and quick to react to everything." About 20 percent of all children can be classified in this way. This child is intensely perceptive, "easily overwhelmed by high levels of stimulation, sudden changes, and the emotional distress of others."[1] These children may also be deep thinkers, empathetic, imaginative, and have the tendency to cry often.

Highly sensitive children will require more support, nurturance, and patience. Maureen Healy, author of *Growing Happy Kids: How to Foster Inner Confidence, Success, and Happiness*, explains that the key to parenting an HSC is to teach the child "how to see their sensitivity as a strength and begin empowering themselves with tools to tap into the upside of their sensitivity such as insight, creativity, and empathy while simultaneously learning how to manage their rich emotional lives."[2]

One of the ways parents can empower their children, especially highly sensitive children, is by preparing them for life's setbacks and inevitable tough times. Have you heard of the terms "lawn-mower parent" and "helicopter parent"? These are parents who mow down any obstacle in their child's way or lift them out and away from their troubles. We do our children a disservice if we try to shield them from the difficult, sad, or painful realities of life. Examples of typical tween and teen setbacks can be not making the cut for a sports team, failing a test, or not getting invited to a party. We need to prepare our children for these experiences, teach them resiliency, and instruct them in ways to cope with their hurt feelings. If your child is HSC, acknowledge that he or she may process these moments more deeply than their peers, and that is ok. Teach them how to put things in perspective. Share with them healthy ways to process their feelings, through identifying and speaking about their feelings. Reassure your child that we all feel overwhelmed by setbacks and hardships at times. We need to emphasize nothing is worth taking your own life. Through honest and open discussions, your child will begin to feel empowered rather than hopeless, when he or she is faced with the realities of life.

Another essential conversation to have with your sensitive child is how to cope when they experience heartbreak. This topic can be discussed in the context of love interests, but also rejection by a peer group. Rejection is, by far, the most painful human experience next to the death of a loved one. As humans, we all crave relationships, acceptance, and love by others. Too often we have seen the consequence of rejection play out tragically in school shootings across our nation. These individuals were often rejected, isolated, and marginalized by their peers or a love interest. Many of these kids who were suffering from this deep pain end up completing suicide. The earlier we discuss and prepare our children for the reality of a broken heart or not being accepted by others, the more we will have done to prevent these tragedies. We need to build up children's stamina and resiliency to weather these moments.

I believe Ryan was a highly sensitive child. By now, I hope I have painted the picture of him as being an adorable, empathetic, and sensitive boy. I would have never changed these characteristics because they are what made him so lovable. However, knowing what I *now* know and seeing this common thread among many other children who have committed suicide, I would have paid much more attention to this trait in him. I would have spent a lot more time building up his resiliency and coping skills, knowing his sensitivity would make him more vulnerable. Although we did get Ryan a counselor, the emphasis was on the bullying rather than taking a holistic approach for his sensitive nature. Additionally, I wish I had prepared him for the inevitable rejection by a love interest. I just didn't think this was going to happen so early in his adolescent life.

As I look back on my own life, I realize how I was impacted by my first heartbreak. I was a senior in high school, feeling rejected and struggling with depression. What has stuck with me since then was a profound moment and turning point during my high school art class one morning with my all-time favorite Catholic high school teacher. Sister Mary Laurena Cullen was the kind of teacher who made you feel comfortable in her classroom. She took the time to get to know me and all of her students. On this particular morning, she came into the classroom with tears running down her face. She went on to tell us that she just learned a former student had died by suicide. She said, "Kids, please don't ever forget this. You can always turn an inkblot into a butterfly. You can always turn a mistake into a lesson learned or a bad situation into something good." Unfortunately, I never got around to sharing this profound lesson with Ryan, but through *Ryan's Story*, I've been blessed with the opportunity to share it with you and with millions of students worldwide.

RESOURCES

Ryan's Story.
http://www.ryanpatrickhalligan.org/resources.htm.

National Suicide Prevention Lifeline.
https://suicidepreventionlifeline.org/. 1-800-273-8255.

American Foundation for Suicide Prevention. "Risk
Factors and Warning Signs." https://afsp.org/about-
suicide/risk-factors-and-warning-signs/.

Aron, Elaine N. *The Highly Sensitive Child.* New York:
Random House, 2002. https://hsperson.com/.

Centers for Disease Control and Prevention. "Suicide
Among Youth."
https://www.cdc.gov/healthcommunication/toolstemplat
es/entertainmented/tips/SuicideYouth.html.

Connecticut Suicide Advisory Board.
http://www.preventsuicidect.org/.

Healy, Maureen. *Growing Happy Kids: How to Foster Inner Confidence, Success, and Happiness.* Deerfield Beach, Florida: HCI, 2012.
https://growinghappykids.com/.

Kersting, Thomas. *Disconnected: How to Reconnect our Digitally Distracted Kids.* 2016.
http://tomkersting.com/.

Mobile Crisis Intervention Services. "Did You Know?"
https://www.empsct.org/information/.

Twenge, Jean M. *iGen: Why Today's Super-Connected Kids Are Growing Up Less Rebellious, More Tolerant, Less Happy – and Completely Unprepared for Adulthood – and What That Means for the Rest of Us.* New York: Simon and Schuster, 2017.
http://www.jeantwenge.com/.

Youth Suicide Warning Signs.
https://www.youthsuicidewarningsigns.org/youth.

AFTERWORD

As a New York City middle school principal for the past twelve years, I have learned the importance of having a strong social-emotional program that supports all students. Creating a safe learning environment will increase student attendance and academic achievement. Culture and climate is everything! Thanks to John Halligan's presentation of Ryan's Story we have created that kind of climate in our school.

Bullying has existed from the beginning of time. With the internet explosion over the past twenty years, bullying has expanded into many shapes and forms. Cyberbullying has become a global epidemic and needs to be dealt with in a proactive manner. It exists in elementary school, middle schools, high schools, colleges, work places, religious institutions, local, state and federal governments.

When I heard about John Halligan's powerful student and parent presentation, *Ryan's Story*, I knew I had to have him speak in our community. Mr. Halligan tells his heartbreaking story about his son as a middle schooler who was bullied, suffered from depression, and ultimately completed suicide. This moving presentation has become the cornerstone of our comprehensive anti-bullying program since 2008.

In 2008, I declared war on cyberbullying and all forms of bullying in the Intermediate School 228 School Community! Since then we have had *Ryan's Story* presented at our school every two years. The impact on our students and parents has been profound. The number of inappropriate behavioral incidents declined and daily school attendance is over 96 percent. More students are becoming upstanders, as Mr. Halligan advises, instead of being bystanders witnessing inappropriate behavior. It's 2019 and we are winning the war on bullying!

John Halligan is a special member of our family and *Ryan's Story* has become a lifesaver for our school community. With the release of the book, *Ryan's Story*, John Halligan can now reach even more parents with tips on bullying, suicide prevention, and safe technology use along with his inspirational message.

Dominick A. D'Angelo
Principal
Intermediate School 228 – David A. Boody
Brooklyn, New York

ABOUT THE AUTHORS

John Halligan is an internationally renowned presenter on bullying and suicide prevention throughout the United States, Canada, and Latin America. He has appeared on *Oprah*, *CBS Morning Show*, *CNN*, *Inside Edition*, *Good Morning America*, *Primetime with Diane Sawyer*, *PBS Frontline*, and radio programs including NPR and the BBC World Radio. John has also received several awards for his work including:

- IBM's Community Service Award, 2005
- Kids Safe Collaborative Community Service Award, 2008
- United Way's Hometown Hero Award, 2008
- Children Abuse Prevention Services Community Award, 2011
- The FBI Director's Community Service Award, 2010
- The Learning Channel Give A Little Award, 2017

In 2004, Mr. Halligan spearheaded the Vermont Bullying Prevention law in honor of his son Ryan. In

2006, he then led the passing of a law which requires education about suicide prevention in public schools. Since 2005, John has visited over 2000 middle and high schools, reaching over a million students with Ryan's Story. If you are interested in having John speak at your child's school, please visit www.RyanPatrickHalligan.org for more information.

johnhalligan@ryansstory.org

Emily B. Dickson has dedicated the past sixteen years to working as a Certified School Counselor in a middle school in Connecticut. Her passion for profoundly understanding and helping students and parents through the trying middle school years has brought her much satisfaction and pride. Having her bachelor's in psychology, master's in counseling and community psychology, and sixth year in school counseling, she has vast experience working with the middle school population, as well as working as a Clinical Case Coordinator at a residential school in Connecticut. Emily is also a mother of two children, ages eight and eleven, and knows first-hand the challenges of navigating in a world where social media has taken over.

emilybethdickson@yahoo.com

NOTES

8. Lessons Learned

1. Centers for Disease Control and Prevention, "Suicide Among Youth," last modified September 15, 2017, https://www.cdc.gov/healthcommunication/toolstemplates/ entertainmented/tips/SuicideYouth.html.
2. Mobile Crisis Intervention Services, "Did You Know?," https://www.empsct.org/information/.

10. They Were Sensitive Too

1. Dr. Elaine Aron, *The Highly Sensitive Child* (New York: Random House, 2002).
2. Maureen Healy, "The Highly Sensitive Child," *Psychology Today* blog, June 1, 2011, https://www.psychologytoday.com/us/blog/creative-development/201106/the-highly-sensitive-child.